ANXIOUS UBER DRIVER

THE GENESIS OF A HUSTLER

PAUL MCKNIGHTON

ISBN-13: 9798644892167

Cover design by: Art Painter
Library of Congress Control Number: 2018675309
Printed in the United States of America

I dedicate this book to my younger self. Great start and continue evolving.

"Our evolution depends on our memory. If we keep forgetting the mistakes of the past, only to keep repeating them, then we will never change."

SUZY KASSEM

CONTENTS

PREFACE

I wrote this book to give insight to those that are "running" and do not know it. I wrote it to help those who come from environments of trauma and poverty and aren't aware of its' influences in their decision making.

INTRODUCTION

A study shows that only 56 out 135, 000 actors actually become famous.

I do not want to sell dope! I had given up the world of hustling to take on a career in the military. After the military I decided to give Hollywood a shot. After the military my life had no meaning. I didn't know who I was, and I no longer had a title. Hollywood provided a way to disguise the anxiety that surfaced upon my discharge.

There are many Veterans and other starving artists that need some type of income to survive. A regular job won't cut it due to the fact that when you get "the call" you need to be available. What was the answer for me?

Uber, provided an excellent opportunity for income and it gave me a chance to serve again. I got to
experience many parts of the city. I had the pleasure of meeting many people whom I wouldn't have under normal circumstances. I had many adventures, fun times, and scary times. I got to know some of the ways the city and traffic works. I learned some of the ins and outs of how to take advantage to get more money. I faced temptation from my past and learned a lot about myself.

CHAPTER I

THE BEGINNING

What the fuck do I got to do to get some money around here!? I shouldn't have left the South or gotten out of the military to chase this pipe dream/fairytale of making it big in LA. These are some of my thoughts while living in Los Angeles after getting out of the military three years ago. I didn't know at the time that I was running from something and instead of going home upon my discharge I wanted to give Hollywood a shot.

Upon my discharge I was diagnosed by a psychiatrist at the VA Hospital with severe anxiety. Many veterans have it and it's not from war contrary to what many civilians would think. It's more from not having an identity and not knowing who you are without your name, rank, and billet description. Many try to stay in the military as long as they can, some get out and go back to what they know before they joined and others go to similar professions such as the police, CIA, FBI etc. But as for me I chose acting, but for the 3 years I been out of the military I've been unsuccessful.

I should just take my Black ass back to Texas. Hell, the rent is cheaper and you get more bang for your buck! But I could not do that. Where I'm from it's a small town and everyone that went to college or the military and came back were branded as failures. So many thoughts and emotions are running through my head and heart at the same damn time. Never had I been in such a state of not knowing what to do. My rent is due, I owe child support, family needs money, and I need money to date, go out, and fuck around with. After days upon days of sitting around feeling sorry for myself, I have to have a man to man talk with myself. I have to sit back, self-reflect, reevaluate, get myself together, and take time organizing a new plan.

What could a brother do to bring in some extra money every month? What can I do for a short amount of time at night or around my auditions? I like background acting and extra work. It fills a void of being out of the military. Having some form of a description of who I am lessens my anxiety. Being an actor gives me a title, something I could swap out for my name, rank, and military title. But acting isn't paying the bills, at least not enough to live and have a freezer full of meat, as we say in Texas.

After days of being in this state my phone rings and everything changes. It's my Big Homie, Mr. Sam Chase! I met Big Sam in the hood of South-Central LA. Big Sam was a real street gangster that was big time in the 80s and 90s during the gangs and the crack epidemic. He went to prison in the 90s for 10 years. He now hustles everything from cars from the car auctions, real estate, and security gigs. He's never going back to prison; Big Sam now invests his money and even does small ventures such as recycling. Big Sam looks as if he was homeless if you saw him, which is funny because he has about four or five thousand dollars cash in his pocket every time I see him.

I answer the phone, and there's this deep raspy voice saying, "What up, man?"

"Nothing much on my end," I state. "What's good with you, OG?"

"Say man, I got another hustle for you," he says with excitement.

"Shit, I'm all for it. What's up?"

"It's this shit called Uber! My cousin's wife does that shit, and she is making about a G a week." (A G is short for a Grand meaning a thousand.)

"For real?" I say. This shit is right on time. "Ok OG, I'm going to check it out! Thanks, and One Love."

As soon as I hung up, I go straight to the internet and check it out. Right away I sign up and upload copies of my license. I upload my registration, proof of insurance, and my selfie. I do all this from my phone, believe it or not! I also had to give information for a background check. Fuck! This is where the momentum starts to go down. I got a fucking DUI about 6 years ago when I was in the Army! Is that shit is going to affect my background check?

Damn, I know one thing: once you start something new, you must use the momentum you have to hold you through. Negative thoughts will creep up to take what you don't even know you are getting yet. It was over 6 years ago, and if that's enough for disqualification, then who the hell is driving? Morgan Freeman?

I continue filling out my information all while thinking they're going to have to disqualify my ass. I sure as hell am not going to disqualify my damn self. Besides, they didn't ask me for my driving history. They asked for my information so they can check my driving history.

My car is ok and runs well. It's a 2006 Cadillac CTS black on black. The gas isn't the best, but it'll do. I got almost a hundred thousand miles on this thing, but it's almost paid for.

First, let me do the math on this shit! Between gas and maintenance, is this Uber shit worth it? Here I go again stopping the momentum and thinking myself out of it. Whatever the math adds up to, I will see for myself and then re-evaluate. Doing something and finding out for yourself is never a waste of time so go ahead and try the thing. It's worth a shot. It's not like I'm getting major roles right now. Getting an oil change and tire rotation is only about $60 bucks, and I get the high mileage mid-grade, which isn't too bad. But little did I know, now I would be getting an oil change with tire rotation every 4 to 6 weeks for the next 3 years.

CHAPTER II

I DIDN'T CHOSE UBER, UBER CHOSE ME!

So after over two months of being hesitant and uninspired to drive, I begin losing the momentum I had before. Finally, I decide to at least fiddle around with the app and fill out my banking information. That way, at least when I do decide to drive, things would be set up already. All I have to do decide to stop procrastinating. But negative thoughts begin to spring up like weeds and destroy my garden of new endeavors.

I'm hungry, and I'm driving to get some food one sunny day. I decide to pull over and familiarize myself some more with the Uber App. I pull over to the side of the road (putting safety first) in Studio City next to some apartments. I proceed and continue filling out the banking information. After completing that, I play around with it some more. I discover a map of where the highest demand for drivers is. The areas around Universal Studios and Hollywood are all highlighted. I decide to hold off on driving for now and continue to get some food.

As I make it halfway down the block, there's a dead end and I'm forced to turn around. I hear a loud noise coming from the app. I tap it thinking I was turning the app off or at least making the beeping noise stop. Completing my U-turn, I turn around and go back through the way I came. Out of nowhere I hear someone screaming, "Hey, I'm right here!"

Looking to my left, there was a guy with his luggage jogging toward the car. At first, I was like *what the hell*, but then he states (while breathing hard) "you're Tyrone, right?" I nod and he says "For David, correct?"

I look down at the app and say, "Yes, for David."

He says "You got my destination?"

"One second, let me double-check." I use common sense and hit start trip, and it has LAX as the destination. So, I state, "LAX, correct?" with confidence.

He answers, "Yes, correct. Southwest terminal one."

During the ride to LAX, David and I have a conversation about the fun we've both had on set as extras. David is a musician from Portland. He plays bass guitar in a band playing in and around the Valley.

Arriving at the airport, I make sure and ask him again if it's Southwest terminal one, and he confirms. Lucky for me, Southwest Airlines is the first terminal in LAX, so I didn't have to fight too much traffic. Note: United has a cut off, and you don't have to drive completely around the entire airport to exit.

David exits the car with his luggage and says, "Thanks man. You are welcome to come to drink and see me play sometimes."

I end the trip and see that I earned $26. *Well damn! What the Fuck happened!?* I look back at it and try searching for an answer to what I had done. I must have turned the Uber app on while putting in my banking information or while I was familiarizing myself with the app. I could have turned it on while looking at those hotspots. Somehow, by luck or chance, I ended up getting a rider going to LAX in the same apartment building I pulled over next to. What are the odds? Being hesitant and uninspired to drive at first, killing my momentum with procrastination to fill out my information, I finally opened the app, and I end up picking up someone at the exact building I pulled over next to. I'm in it to win it now! Plus, I got $26 bucks! After getting paid, my inspiration and momentum to drive has come back.

CHAPTER III

GAINING EXPERIENCE

Beep! The Uber app goes off again! It looks like I'm headed to Marina Del Rey. I get to Washington street and the app says take a left on Via Marina. Damn, it's a lot of traffic over here, but it's hella eye candy walking around as well. Make my left on Via Marina, and there's this fine young lady in yoga pants and a tank top walking some little dog. Man, I hope she is my rider! Sure, enough she waves me down and I pull over.

"Tyrone?" she asks.

I say, "Hell yeah, baby. The one and only." No, joking, I say, "Yes, I am" and ask if she is Stacy. She was.

"Is it ok if my dog comes with me?"

"Hell yeah! I mean, sure, you're fine. I mean, the dog is fine." I start the trip, and it looks as if she is only going right down the street to a place called Moda Yoga. I didn't mind since she was fine, but I wonder why the hell didn't she walk? Like, aren't you into fitness and shit? So, I drop her off, and I'm thinking she must be one of the instructors. Who else could have had a dog while training? She could have walked and made it here before I did. Someone was riding their bike next to us the entire trip. While driving from her building to her destination, he was passing me at every stoplight. $4 total for the trip? I'll take it.

Next trip is to the Marriott. I pull up, and there's eight fucking bags, two badass kids (not judging, I will state why in the following paragraph), and their mom. I place the big ones in the trunk first and squeeze a couple of small ones in also.

"I will ride with this one in my lap," states the mother of the family. The father comes out from the hotel gets in and sits up front with me.

The kids have already begun to fight over which seat they want. Then they start going at it again over which seatbelt was theirs. I start the trip, and I'm going to LAX. I start driving, and they are getting frustrated being in the back seat with their mother and the luggage. They are so restless and jumpy that one of them starts kicking the middle console. *Watch out you, little fucker* is what I want to say, but I keep my composure. Later, one starts crying and saying that they want to eat their Takis and that they are in one of the bags in the back.

"I can pull over if you need me too," I state, hoping to God that she said no!

"Oh, no," says the mother. "We must get to the airport. They can eat when we get out. Hey, guys calm down!" The mother tries to settle them down. "Sorry," she says to me.

What the fuck is that smell? Did one of these little kids shit themselves? Unless it was the mother? How in the hell is everyone acting like they don't smell this shit? Finally, one of the kids says to his mother that he farted. The dad looked embarrassed, but I was happy that the kid said something. I could let their window down now and not feel uncomfortable about it.

So I'm in traffic, listening to these kids yelling, fighting, and complaining. They're kicking the middle armrest, and in the meantime, I'm smelling their farts. I don't know if I'm cut out for this shit, but I don't want to start talking myself out of this again. I have already gotten over the procrastination from starting in the first place.

Finally, the Dad yells "Calm down!" and then the child stops kicking the middle armrest. At last, silence.

That was easy. It appears the children do whatever the fuck they feel until the father says something. If that's the case, why the fuck didn't he say something in the first place? Do you mean to tell me that all this time, all the father had to do was speak up? Am I being too serious and overthinking it?

But these kids have their parents trained, they do whatever they want until they hear their daddy's voice. The father says sorry and I say oh it's no problem they're being kids. I say that being nice, knowing damn well I can't wait to drop their asses of at the airport. It's interesting how anxiety works, being that's what my diagnosis was once out of the military. I forgot about it for a while. I dealt with it by avoiding crowded places, etc. I didn't think it would catch up with me while doing this, but it has. I should take my medication before driving.

I get to the airport, and it's like New York and China put together, and they're going to the worst terminal. Terminal four is around the airport with no shortcuts. Unlike terminal seven United, or the shortcut to five, which you can get immediately over to the end of six if you're good enough.

Finally, I arrive at terminal four American Airlines. Get the fuck out is all on my mind but I say, "Here you guys go!" But I forgot about all the luggage. I had to help them with the trunk. I help grab the mother's bag out of her lap and help with the rest out of the trunk. Oh, shit! I must end the trip!

End trip for a total of $11. Wait a minute, I have been through hell with these little kids. Driving them while they were farting, whining, kicking, and yelling. The fact that I loaded all that luggage for a total of only $11 and some change. I had to look at the trip details to figure out how in the hell I only got $11 for that trip. Trip details state that from the Marriot to Lax was only 6.6 miles. Man, fuck this! I have been out here in the hot ass traffic for over 2 hours for less than $40. But hey, that's over $15 per hour. Something is better than nothing, and I'm optimistic about it getting greater later.

Note to self: when doing airport runs, make sure to know exactly what terminal to drive to first. If it's terminal six or seven, make sure to get into the far-left lane immediately to make the terminal six and seven exits. In traffic, this will save a lot of time.

Deet. The app goes off again while I'm trying to get out of LAX. Back to terminal four. *I could have stayed there,* I say to myself. I keep driving thinking *I hope these muthafuckas are going somewhere far.* I hope they are going to somewhere like Rancho Cucamonga so I can get some mileage. I pull over at the terminal pickup point and profile who Stephanie may be. Stephanie could be anyone. She could be Black, White, or Asian.

But before I could get any good looks, I hear "Hey, are you Tyrone?"

I look, smile, and say "Yes, you're Stephanie, right"? She has yoga pants. I'm going back to Marina Del Rey. Although it's only 11 bucks, it's still an earning opportunity.

I start the trip, and she's going to Santa Monica. **Deet**. Wait a minute, I already have a rider?

Stephanie says, "You may be picking up someone else. I'm in a pool. Let me check she says yes you are picking up Dexter."

A pool? What's that? I look at the app and see another rider added at terminal seven. *This going to be nice,* I thought to myself. *Wonder where he is going?*

I get to terminal seven and pick up Dexter, who has one bag and one carry on. I get the trunk.

"Thanks brother," says Dexter, a tall brother with dreads and glasses.

I start the trip, and it only states where Stephanie is going, which in Santa Monica. I continue to the 405 South, and as soon as I get on the 405 freeway, **Deet,** the app goes off again. *Damn, I'm going to have 3 riders,* I say to myself as I exit to pick up the 3rd rider. I hear a sound that I haven't heard before. I look at my app and it says rider canceled. Muthafucka! I'm in all this traffic with two riders and get off the freeway to have this guy cancel. Why am I getting disturbed by this? I don't want to let a rider that canceled on me make the ride unpleasant for Stephanie and Dexter. Plus, they can more than likely see it on my face. I remind myself that I'm in this for the long haul, and that I'm sure cancellations come with driving for Uber. So, I continue and keep it moving.

The app goes off again, and this time I exit Santa Monica Blvd. It's a couple? The app states that it's only one rider, but I don't care, and I don't believe the other riders are too concerned. (I should have asked them?)

"Hey, get in where you fit in. One in the front and one in the back."

The guy gets in the front, and his girlfriend in the back with Steph and Dexter. The guy appears to have an attitude. I ask his name, and he doesn't say shit. So, I ask again, this time he nods and says with an attitude, "it's on the app." Fucking asshole! How the hell do I know it's you, first of all, and is the ride for her or you? But I kept my thoughts to myself and continued the trip to Santa Monica to drop Stephanie off.

Arriving at a nice apartment complex on 5th ave, I drop off Stephanie and end her trip. I can't help but be curious about why this guy next to me appears to have an attitude. He keeps fidgeting around in his seat as if he is uncomfortable. There is plenty of room in this Cadillac. It is roomier than the little ass Priuses that most riders are usually riding in. At least that's the most I've seen all while at the airport, Priuses and black SUVs. I drop the couple off next to the ocean on Ocean Ave.

Dexter is next, and this thing is already going off again. I should have known I wouldn't make it off Ocean Ave. without another rider added. It's live over here.

Dexter opens up and says "Ol' boy didn't want his woman sitting next to a brother. Plus, he felt uncomfortable riding with you."

Oh well. His ass could have canceled like the person before him did. I knew it was something I said, but it could have been a lot of things. He could be uncomfortable with me as a driver. There was a car full of five people, including me, which could have been the catalyst. He also was aware that he was to be by himself and should've paid extra for his girlfriend. He could have been having a bad day. Bottom line, my job is to get him from point A to point B and to get him there safe. I see this gig incorporates some professionalism, critical thinking, mindfulness, and street smarts. I'm up to it, so let's keep it moving.

CHAPTER IV

DRIVING MODELS

After driving for a few months, meeting, and parlaying with other drivers, I learned a lot while waiting on LAX arrivals. I was able to discover different strategies that people use to amass funds while driving. There are many different strategies, times, and the reasons why people drive. To my knowledge, many of the drivers fit into the following categories. The breakdown goes like this:

The Early Risers. The early riser strategy has an emphasis on the airport runs. The more seasoned drivers even go as far as calling it a track (I will explain this later). This strategy is for those who want to get ahead of traffic and start around 4-6 am. The Early Riser Strategy is to post up in front of hotels and end up at LAX. Although there are other places you may end up. You may pick up someone going to work, or you may pick up someone who has been partying and calling it a night/day. If picking up the later, it is important that you either crack a window or have an air freshener. This will help ensure the next rider isn't smelling the odors.

I make sure to not accept any more requests when having malodorous riders in my vehicle. This is for several reasons. First, it's to give me time to clean and air out the vehicle before picking anyone up. Next, the rider doesn't have any way of determining where the alcohol smell in the vehicle is from. Believe it or not, they can suspect you of driving while under the influence. I don't think I need to explain how that can go bad.

This happened to a few drivers that I know. It does not matter if the rider felt the driver was under the influence or they were full of shit. The thing to do if you suspect the driver to be under the influence would be to ask the driver to let you out of the vehicle. Once out of the vehicle then you contact the police. Do not ride the entire trip and then report the driver. The fact that they did is how a few of the drivers got their driving privileges reinstated.

After dropping off a rider or riders that smell, a good way to deal with odors is to drive on the freeway with all the windows down. Do this for an exit or two to air out the vehicle before picking up the next rider. Vacuuming the car also helps, so keep quarters in your car or invest in a small portable vacuum. This not only works for the after-party crowd, but it also works for riders who have been eating out. Also this works if you fart, belch, or have riders with food in your vehicle. If the weather or the comfort of the rider requires the window to stay closed, I immediately do not accept any more trips. this ensures there aren't any riders getting in immediately afterward. I then find a safe place to pull over, vacuum, and wipe my seats down with leather wipes. After that, I start accepting new riders, and by the time I arrive, they have a fresh car to get inside. Freshness and a little cleanliness plus consideration go a long way. I have received plenty of compliments and 5-star ratings on cleanliness alone. I'm sure there are plenty of other ways to deal with car odors, but that's what's effective for me.

Being an early riser, it is important to have bottled water and gum. For your riders (especially the partiers), early morning breath is common. It's important to understand that there is an element of trust involved in the trip. Many riders are suspicious when it comes to drinking out of plastic bottles.

I discovered this when I ended up consuming the majority of the bottled water that I purchased. I could understand if the bottled water was a cheap brand, but this bottled water was only of the top named bottles. Bottles like Fiji and Voss, where you pay $6 or $7 bucks in the nightclub. After realizing people and/or the bottles were suspect, I decided to place La Croix canned water in the back. After making that move, I couldn't keep water in my vehicle. People were taking extras upon exiting the vehicle.

An important strategy to note as an Early Riser is to park in front of hotels and get a good airport run. Me being in the Valley, my strategy is to turn my app on as soon as I leave my apt. in Studio City around 4-5 am. I always accept the first trip no matter what. This is to get into the shit (meaning get started to where the trips are coming back to back and you are driving nonstop).

If I get an LAX run, one strategy for Early Risers is to drop off the rider and head to the LAX rideshare parking lot. Then, you get in the queue for new LAX arrivals. This could be positive or negative. It's up to the driver to play it and weigh the options. Due to long wait times, when you get a rider, they may not be going anywhere but to Marina Del Rey, Venice, or Inglewood. This could limit your money. Parking in the LAX queue could affect riders more than drivers. When drivers are in the queue, they don't want to lose their position. So when there is a rider that lives near the airport, most drivers cancel. This makes it difficult for the riders in the morning when they live near LAX.

The positive side of waiting in the parking lot is that someone could be flying to LAX and going to Orange County. This is worth the wait if you plan to continue driving to make your way back up in that traffic. One more strategy of the Early Risers is to do what some seasoned drivers call to run the track. Running the track goes like this:

After you drop off your rider at LAX, continue exiting the airport. With luck, you didn't get any other trips before leaving the airport. Turn off your app and do not accept any more trips. Then you get back on the 405 freeway and go north. Do not go south because there isn't that much mileage and the odds are you are going to have a rider in Manhattan Beach. When you get a rider going from Manhattan Beach to the LAX, you will come right back using Sepulveda for a small fare. If you go 405 North, you can continue a further distance. Continue at least to the 10 freeway. Once you are at the 10 freeway exit, turn your app back on. After turning your app back on, you can go east toward DTLA, west toward Santa Monica, or keep going straight picking up riders around UCLA. The odds are at that time in the morning, you will be heading back to LAX. You repeat this several times over and over again, hence it's called running the track.

The reason for this is that the odds of someone going to LAX are higher. The reason to not turn your app on before the 10 freeway is your fair is going to be less than $10. To ensure that you don't have an airport run from Inglewood or Culver City, drivers skip these areas. They skip these areas by either turning their apps off or flat out canceling the trip. This is one of the many reasons why people that live next to the airport find it hard to get a ride.

Along with not wanting to give up their position in the queue to pick up someone nearby, some riders park or ride around the high-end hotels in Los Angeles like the Four Seasons. They do this hoping to pick up a celebrity. At the very least, the idea is that if you don't get to pick up a celebrity, the rider is wealthy. Doing this increases the chances of receiving a healthy tip! Other Early Risers start early so they can finish by lunch. Start early so you can finish early and have the rest of the day to do what you want.

Lunch to 5 Crew. This strategy is in horrible traffic, but it works for those who work it. The Lunch to 5 Crew is waking up or starting to drive around 11 or noon. Many drivers during this time think that the early morning is too early to start driving. Some got off a night shift job around 7 am and got a few hours rest before driving. One downside to this time is they end up finishing smack dead in midday traffic. You could start earlier at 9 am or 10 and get more hours before rush hour. If you choose that option, it is there for you. If you're married or in a relationship, this might work for you. This will work because you are home when everyone else is getting home after school and work. One other way this timing is good is that it at lunchtime, many people are already where they are going. People are either going to lunch or not too far from where they want to go. This can keep you in the same area you started if you decide that you may want to stay around the same area. This works for some and doesn't for others. To each his own.

The Evening Crew. This time is the worst and most stressful in my own opinion. These motivated individuals start in the middle of rush hour traffic. This is crazy to me, but the person most likely has a day job and drives right after work. It could be the only time they can drive. A positive way to look at it is that if starting in 5 o'clock traffic, the traffic only gets better. The more you drive, the more the traffic lessens. This will at least give you a nice drive home upon finishing. You also will have trips back to back to back, and you will be making money. But the time fighting in traffic is too stressful for me and my anxiety. Another negative to this strategy is that if you have a tough job, you may need to wash up a little before driving. But if you have a desk job that's relaxed, then you're ok. It takes longer to get from point A to point B when driving in traffic.

The wear and tear on your vehicle, especially the tires and brakes, is far worse. You get less gas mileage, and even if there is a surge, it may not be worth it. It takes a lot longer for trips, and you get paid more for mileage and not for time. This isn't a good time to drive if you have anxiety or if you are an anxious person like myself.

The best method of driving during this time (as far as I know) is to not give a fuck about time or being in any certain area. Be cool and get there when you get there all while being safe. Most accidents also happen midday, so you must be an exceptional defensive driver. Good Luck!

Nighttime Drivers are those that more than likely have a day job and want to supplement their income. The Nighttime Drivers also consist of those that don't have "real jobs" such as actors, musicians, and other artists. You have your professional drivers. These are the drivers with the black SUVs, luxury black sedans, and town cars with the TCP numbers. These guys make good money by transporting groups of people. Some people want to spend a little more money for their comfort. They may have an event or a night out at the club. Many escorts, strippers, and celebrities all use these vehicles. It's also a go-to for many basketball and large football players. Where else could they fit besides in an SUV? Another group of people that drive currently at night is your party people. Unfortunately, some of these drivers are driving to get lucky with the ladies. Some are trying to recoup some of the money they blew in the club. Some are your addicts and creeps. You can cash out your funds, and then you can support your drug habit. You could drive all night and continue making more money to get high. Their drug of choice is more than likely coke or meth.

It's important to understand that there are many other reasons to drive. People could be driving due to losing their job. Some might find that Uber pays more than where they currently work. Some drive because of the freedom in the opportunity of working when they want to work. Seniors and other retired individuals find it as something to do in their spare time. Some drivers enjoy being around people.

The driving times are not set in stone, and you can drive anytime you want. For example, you can have an early riser go until lunch. You could have an evening driver go until nighttime. You could be a nighttime driver and drive until the early riser time frame. I chose to drive at night after weighing the positives and negatives of driving at all the other times.

The positives of driving at night are a lack of traffic and a smoother drive. Less traffic is better for your vehicle's wear and tear. You get better gas mileage. Your tires and brakes last longer.

This causes you to have fewer expenditures on vehicle repairs.

Who drives when? It all depends on the person and the person's situation. You do what is best for you.

The negatives to driving at night are all the drunk and high individuals. Especially the ones that don't conduct themselves and are rude. It can become rather difficult trying to pick up someone when the club lets out. There are hundreds of people outside with their cellphones lit up, and it can be confusing. Thus making it difficult to pick up your rider.

There are a plethora of illegal activities. You have people scoring drugs, people that have stolen something and hop in the Uber as if it's a getaway car. You have people cheating on their partners. Riders will request that you end the trip, giving it an appearance that you dropped them of someplace. Only after ending the trip, they will pay you cash to take them somewhere else. Somewhere else could be to get a hooker, go to the casino, or the strip club. Doing it this way works for them if their spouse/partner has access to the Uber app. He or she can see all the trip information.

Hollywood is not the safest city in LA. But you are taking people back home, and they may live in some dangerous neighborhoods. So there must be some caution in different "hoods" dropping riders off. People fall asleep in the back seat especially in the back of a Cadillac. But you must wake them up upon arrival to their destination. This can be tricky, and it's not as easy as it seems. First, is the rider male or female? If the rider is male, then a simple "hey bro" and a possible nudge on the shoulder will work. If not, then you will have to exit the vehicle and open his door and try and wake him up with a shake and louder tone. This isn't the same for women, and the women seem to pass out the worst! With her you will have to roll her window down and make sure she is up upon arrival. If she isn't up upon arrival from the air cool air blowing in from the window, I try turning the music up. After that, I raise my tone to get her attention. After that, I drive her ass to the nearest police station. This has happened to me before and I will explain.

One night, I was on the West-Side of LA between Venice and Santa Monica. I got a trip that was a 1.5 surge at a bar called The Whaler. Once I arrived, several women surrounded my car asking me if I was Tyrone and if I was here for Riley. I verified with them that I was Tyrone and asked them to hop on in. They weren't getting in; they stated and that the ride was for their friend. They all pointed towards their drunk friend who was being carried out. *Sure, no problem*, I thought at the time. They struggle to finally get her in the car, close the door, and I begin towards her destination.

For a few minutes, I'm driving and begin to look at the trip's destination. Wait a damn minute; Sharky's in Manhattan Beach!? It's after 1:30 am, and I'm pretty sure she has had enough to drink. I ask Riley where she stays so I can update her address in the app, and there is no response. I look back and she is back there passed the hell out. I yell, "Riley what is your address!?" Still, no response. I'm tempted to drive back to the Whaler. If I do, I'm sure I can hunt down her friends that loaded her in the car.

I turn around and I roll her window down, guessing this cold ass oceanic air would wake her up. After about a block or two of driving back toward the Whaler and calling her name a few more times, finally she wakes up. I proceed to ask her what her address is she instinctively states in on the app. I tell her that Sharky's Bar and Grill Manhattan Beach is what's on the app, not her home address. I didn't know if she lived near there and didn't want to put her real address in or not, because some people do that. She passes back out. I yell out her name and she got up out the back seat and yells what right in my ear. I tell her about Sharky's and that it's the address on her destination. I didn't know if she lived near there or if she had entered her last destination from earlier today. She states shut the fuck up and drive! Are you serious!? That's it for me, and luckily, I had by chance passed the Culver City Police dept.

I immediately turned around, parked, locked the doors, and went inside. Once inside I let the officers know the situation. These guys were prompt and professional. They checked to see if she needed an ambulance. Upon determining that she didn't, they proceeded to ask her where she was going because she was not going to a bar. She gives the officer her address, and the officer asks if it's ok for me to continue taking her. She says ok. The officer looks at me in a way that I understood as I had an awkward ride ahead of me. Long story short, I drop her off at home and guess what? The next day I received a good rating and a tip. Now imagine that. To pick up drunk chicks or to not pick up drunk chicks? That shit could have gone bad, but luckily it didn't.

CHAPTER V

SOLDIER GIRL

In the Hollywood/Studio City area, people are visiting from a distance and you may get long trips. Also, for me, there is something sensual and stimulating when I drive at night. I come alive in the nighttime. I find myself thinking about life and reflect on the past and focus on the future. The painted lines on the wide open freeway stand out at night. When I'm driving inbetween them I get into a meditative state. Sometimes its as if I'm in an alternate reality.

There are some advantages to driving drunk people. Many are friendly. Sometimes drunk riders give away information on investments. Other drunk riders are fun! Some let you know where to find the nightspots, restaurants, and hidden parts of the beaches in Malibu.

When driving during the night, I start in between about 9-11 pm. That's when traffic dies down in LA. I post up at the parking meters on Cahuenga and then turn my app on. This places me in a position to get a trip from Universal Studios. This method of mine works out at least 90 percent of the time. Getting a pick up from Universal Studios is an excellent way to start the night. There are always surges from all the people visiting Universal Studios. Many of the people visiting Universal Studios are also visiting Disneyland. This means it's more than likely that their hotel is down in Anaheim. Over 30 miles plus a surge is some damn good money! If I'm waiting too long at Universal Studios or there's not a surge, I will get on the 101-freeway. I will head south, and I'm sure I will get a hit from a rider before making it to DTLA. Doing things this way is for sure to get me into the shit in Hollywood, and it will be trips back to back from thereon.

The time seems as if it goes by faster at night, especially if you are in the shit in Hollywood. There are so many people out partying. People are eating, drinking, doing drugs, pimping, whoring, and anything else you can think of. Once the nightclubs let out, the entire area is lit with surges. First, you must fight to get to your riders and pick them up. Then after that, it's another fight to get out of the area. People are driving crazy! The drunk people, taxis, the valet drivers, and the other rideshare drivers who can at times be the worst. However; as soon as you get on the freeway, it's smooth sailing. Hit 80, set the cruise, and you can get from Hollywood to Long Beach in 25 minutes. I bullshit you not.

If in Weho, Hollywood, DTLA, etc., the app will give the fastest route. Yet sometimes the riders have their preferred way to get to their destinations. So here is some information that may help get a few more dollars when driving at night when the freeway is wide open. Always ask the rider or riders if they have a route preference. If they say yes, then you drive to their destination with their preferred route. If they say no, then you look at the routes that google maps (which is my preference) provides for you. Google maps will provide a route and will have other similar routes to take, take a similar route that has the furthest mileage.

No, this is not unethical. The riders had no route preference, and you choose the best route for you. What is unethical is if you were to drive out of the way of the rider's destination to add mileage. Let me give you an example. If a rider is going from Hollywood to DTLA, it is unethical to go from Hollywood to the Valley and then turn around and say you forgot a turn. That's very unethical. Missing turns on purpose is unethical. Not ending the trip on time on purpose to get more money is unethical. I hope you understand and exercise the common sense of ethics. You need to exercise common sense if you plan to drive for any rideshare company.

So back to choosing the best routes. Besides choosing a route that has the most mileage, use the one that gets you out of traffic quicker. It's usually the one you make up for yourself to get out of traffic. For example, if a concert has let out at the Palladium on Sunset Blvd, upon arriving to pick up your riders, it's good practice to call and get a clear idea where they're at and what they have on (outfit, glasses, hats, etc.). They may even call you, which is a plus and allows you to pay attention to the road. Once you get through the hell of traffic and get to your riders, you must get out of there the best way you can. The app may recommend U-turns or other turns that may seem impossible. It's up to you to use common sense and get out of there the best way you can. Once out of the shit, you can then proceed as the app suggests. It is important to note that some riders will demand that you go the way they want you to go. This may be difficult at times. A rule of thumb when this happens is to decide if the route they want is unsafe or not. Time-consuming and out of the way difficulties are not a safety hazard. This is something that you must build tolerance for.

I remember one night I was driving in Hollywood. I dropped some passengers off at Roscoe's Chicken and Waffles. After that, I get another hit for a pickup at the Palladium, which is right down the street. The rider contacts me and asks where I am as if I should be there already. I tell her that I will pick her up on Argyle, and ask her to walk to the back so I could pick her up. She agreed. It's easier for me to take Selma and come up the back way. That way is better than to take Sunset. If I take Sunset, I will go through hell to pick her up there or on El Centro, which is where everyone else is waiting.

I make a U-turn on Argyle, park on the side, call the rider again, and let her know I'm here. I look in my rearview and, oh shit, here she comes dragging another young lady with her. She then dumps the drunken young lady in the backseat. She leaves the door open and begins walking back towards the Palladium.

"What the fuck?" I say out loud! "Ma'am, are you going to get in and shut the door?" My first thoughts are to call 911 and tell them that someone dumped and drunk person in the back of my car and left. I think about getting out of the car and going after her, but I will call her on the phone again first. I begin to call her on the phone, I look back, and I'll be damned, she is dragging another drunk chick with her. She loads the other drunk chick in and makes her step over the one that's already in the backseat.

She then gets in the front seat and says, "That's it. Lets go."

What a soldier she was, to me! She packed not one, but two drunk friends in the Uber. I proceed to take them to their destination. Her destination was right around the corner at the 24hr fitness parking lot. While driving, I hear one of her friends trying to open the door, so I lock it. She then starts fiddling around with the door and window buttons and the window itself. I realize she trying to roll the window down and she is more than likely going to throw up. I help her out and I roll the window down for her. I keep driving and start to smell throw up, but I see the riders' head is out of the window as if she is sleep. The worst thing if anything that I am expecting is to wipe off my car on the outside or go through the carwash. I continue driving to the 24-hr. parking garage. I get to fourth-floor parking, and the girl who packed them in says we're parked here on this floor in front of the 24 hr. Fitness entrance. Right about now, I'm expecting to park and wipe vomit off my car. Damn it! Upon exiting the vehicle, I notice that since she is so short, she didn't make it outside the fucking car. Her head only came to the top off the door where the window lets down. She had vomited all inside of the window, door, floor, seat, and outside of the door. I was so fucking pissed. I immediately grab some napkins and towels from the trunk and start wiping shit down, but it's not enough. The chick who packed them in had started to help wipe the seat, but it was useless. The soldier girl wants me to not report anything to Uber since she is helping clean up. I started to take pictures and she then proceeds to give me 30 dollars to not report it. Not enough. Sorry and fuck off!

I drive to the Shell gas station and get paper towels from the window washing stations at the gas pump. I use the towels, the window cleaner, and a t-shirt to clean the car up. Luckily for me I have leather seats, but this shit inside the window opening is hard as fuck to get out. I must wipe inside the door where the window goes up and down and then roll the window up halfway. After the window is up halfway, I must wipe the vomit that comes up out of the door and repeat it to get all the vomit out. I wipe down the leather with leather wipes. I buy an air freshener (new car scent) from inside the Shell gas station, then I go through the carwash. After that, I still must vacuum out the car. This is all during primetime Hollywood night hours. After sending in the pictures to Uber and texting the incident report, I receive a total of $200 for the mishap. Not bad for everything I went through, but I wasn't done for the night.

CHAPTER VI

A CLOSE CALL AND FUCK THE HILLS

When the clubs let out and the maps are lit with surges, a driver's heart rate increases with the chances of earnings. But it can go in many different directions. Many are hoping for the long one going from Hollywood to Long Beach, OC, or even the Valley. I wouldn't mind going to Woodland Hills on a 2.5x surge or higher. Some drivers won't even pick up anyone under a 2.0x surge. My strategy is to pick up anything. I pick up anything because, although the surge may be a 1.7x, they could be going to Long Beach or Santa Clarita for all I know. If the rider is only going to another bar or restaurant in Hollywood, that's good because it's surging all night. If the person is going right outside of the red areas, it's a good method to turn your app off. Don't accept any more riders until you get back to the red areas and then turn your app back on. I have been driving back into the surge area and other Uber drivers are flying past me doing the same thing. I wait until I'm in the middle of the surge area to turn back on. It's possible you could still turn it on right before you get into the red and get lucky. But be careful because the Uber algorithm will sometimes attempt to give you a rider that's outside of the area. This also works like the airport parking queue that I described before. When Hollywood and other areas are surging, many drivers cancel on riders who aren't paying a premium. This does lower your acceptance rating. If you do this often, depending on the misuse, it could cause you to lose bonuses and promotions. If you keep doing it, you could get yourself deactivated. You will also notice that you aren't getting as many trips as you usually do. If you receive many trips outside the surging areas, you can try and turn your app off and on again. You can also suck it up and take the trip outside of the surge area. Remember, some money is better than no money. If you are doing this, or a method like this, it's very important to note as I stated earlier it will affect your rating. One way around this is to accept as many trips as you can back to back. This increases your rating, so when the weekend comes, you can make a few cancellations. The algorithm works to serve the rider not the driver. The algorithm gives the trip to whoever is more of a guarantee for the company. They are going to give the most amount of rides to the person that accepts any trip they give them. Assuming you are in the same places as everyone else, understand that if you are playing games, you're not liked. But if you are the only one around, then you will get the trip more than likely. One way to position yourself to where you increase your earnings is to have two phones. Do this, or turn your app off and turn on the rider app. Once you turn on the rider app, view the map to see where most of the Ubers are. Then position yourself outside of them in a different area. This will help you to avoid crowded competition.

If you are new to driving, the kiss method is the best way of driving. I would recommend that a new driver would start and accept anything thrown at them. Do not get into the hustle part of it all. After driving for a while, the kiss method gets old and I like to get competitive. That's the main reason behind me trying different things. If anything, it keeps me and other drivers from getting bored of driving.

Please understand there are going to be times that you must cancel. Situations like bathroom emergencies or forgetting to turn the app off. You could be no longer driving and at home and feel your app go off (yes this happens). Accidents can happen, especially during the evening and morning traffic. Important phone calls, vehicle failures, and running out of gas are also reasons to cancel. Consider this when you cancel for the promise of a higher payout. This could save you from canceling as much and getting deactivated.

I have had to cancel twice due to vehicle failure. The first was near the airport. I had a pickup on Isis street, and before arriving at the person's apartment, I hit a big ass pothole. I mean it was a huge chunk of street missing that blew out not one but two tires. I called the rider and told them that they needed to cancel. I couldn't cancel after I had already accepted the trip. The app won't let you cancel if you have not reached the destination yet.

The next time I had to cancel, the rider was in the car with me believe it or not! Before driving this night, I had my vehicle serviced at Pep Boys. I took it in for my battery, and they recommended that I use these red and green anti-corrosion washers. Thinking my vehicle was ok to drive, I fill up my tank, go to the gym, eat, shower, and get ready for another night of driving.

It's another busy night, and I'm in DTLA going back and forth from LA Live to USC. I finally get a hit for the JW Marriot. I pick up the rider from the JW Marriot, and luckily for me he is going to the Westside. I'm en route to the rider's destination in Santa Monica. Then out of the blue, while I'm on 110 freeway exiting to the 10 west freeway, my car starts to shut down. The rpm's go to zero, and the entire vehicle starts to lose power. I turn into a professional driver out of nowhere. I state to the driver, "Sir, I'm having a vehicle malfunction."

The rider doesn't hear me, so I talk louder and say, "Sir, I'm going to take this next exit to get off the freeway for safety".

The rider says, "Man, are you for serious? Quit playing." He couldn't believe it. So, I pull over off the freeway.

I tell the rider to go ahead and request another Uber. I let him know that I will contact Uber as well and let them know not to charge him. He was cool about it, so we stood out and waited until his next Uber arrived. I look under my hood once I made sure the rider was good. I see that the battery cable is completely disconnected from the battery terminal. Those washers didn't allow the cables to tighten down on the terminal. Luckily for me, I was able to hand tighten the battery cable myself and make it home safe. I took my vehicle back to Pep Boys, and they said they removed the red and green anti-corrosion washers. They stated that they were sorry and that they used some spray and they tightened everything. Looking back, I should have sued Pep Boys, but oh well. No more money for me that night.

Some nights there are so many trips back to back that you are about to run out of gas. Sometimes, you don't realize it until you have a rider with you and you're en route to their destination. This will mess with your money and will force you to decide while en route. Some riders are assholes and will give you a bad rating. Some will even go as far as contacting Uber support if you make a stop at the gas station, but some riders don't care. You should fill up before driving. You don't know when it's going to be nonstop trips back to back. But you should prepare for it. If on empty, I accept the next trip and stop at the first gas station I see. I get the gas and then proceed. It benefits me to have been in and around Hollywood and the Valley enough to know where everything is.

It is a slow Friday night in LA. I have this very sexy Armenian chic going from Santa Monica to Rocco's Tavern on Ventura Blvd in the Valley. On the way to Rocco's Tavern, I notice I am on empty. When I'm on empty, I usually have a long time until the car will stop running. But this time, I have been driving for so long that it is past empty. I am driving on fumes. I decide that since I know there's a gas station right next to Rocco's Tavern, its ok I will be able to make it. I exit the 405 freeway to Sepulveda. I get to Ventura Blvd and make a right turn. Fuck, I'm nervous. I swear I will never be in this situation again. Should I tell her? No, you're almost there. I'm nervous, and I know she can see me sweating. Oh well, I keep driving. Damn, Rocco's isn't right of the freeway. I could have taken the Woodman exit and did better than this. I have already passed a gas station. I swear, if I run out of gas, I'll crown myself the dummy of the year.

Finally reaching Rocco's Tavern, she is about to get out and decides she wants to talk. Fuck! She says "Hey do you mind waiting here for a second? I don't see my friends".

I say, "Ok cool," but I didn't want to. "I'm going to park over here at the gas station and get gas so I can be out of traffic."

She gets in, and I pull up around to the gas station. What do you know; there is this huge fucking brawl. I mean, these dudes are going at it. They are recording it all at the gas station in front of everyone! My apps going off. I accept the trip because it's right down the street at the One Up Bar. The rider still in the car, but luckily her friends have come out of the bar to meet her. I go to the pump where the fight has cleared, and I squeeze about $10 in and get the fuck out of there. I arrive at the One Up Bar and pick up my next riders like nothing happened.

Note to self: I made sure I had enough gas from that point on. I spent time reflecting on the situation. The bottom line? It was not worth it. The worst thing that could have happened for me being responsible and stopping to get gas, even while with a rider, would only have been a negative rating (assuming the rider gave me one). That doesn't outweigh the worst thing that could have happened. Had I ran out of gas on the freeway, that's an accident and possible death. Playing irresponsible driving at it's finest. That fight was a sign. Wake up!

One other reason for canceling that I forgot to mention was that many people use Uber to go to the emergency room. This is ok if it's not a big emergency but not when you're in a pool!

Driving in the Valley again on a cool random night, I decide to try something different and turn my app on from home. I figure I will take all trips back to back and see where I ended up, although it didn't matter. I end up on Coldwater Canyon, and I get a hit for the Sanamluang Café in North Hollywood. I pick the couple up. The brother is cool, and his girl is fine as hell. He was from Oakland and recommended that when I'm done driving to go inside, check it out, and order a number 31.

I said "Cool, good looking out."

I drop them off and pick up my next rider around Coldwater Canyon and Riverside. I'm outside waiting for about four to five minutes, and the app gives me the option to cancel the rider. I get ready to cancel and receive my free five bucks when the door opens. I hear someone breathing hard. I turn around, and the rider holding her chest and pointing at the app. I immediately, though shaken up a bit, start the trip to see that she is going to the Valley Presbyterian Hospital. I press on the gas not knowing what was wrong with her, but the hospital is only five minutes away. While driving, I get another rider added onto the pool. *God damn you, you mean to tell me you're in a pool?* I keep driving and cancel the next ride. I get the lady to the hospital safe and she runs inside. What was I to do? I ended the trip and drove off.

Luckily for me, now you can cancel, because later pools would be automatic, and you couldn't cancel. Some riders would request that you not pick up the next person. They did this because they were on a schedule or they don't want anyone else riding with them. But this came at the expense of the driver's rating.

In the Hollywood Hills, or any other Hills In Los Angeles, there isn't any good cellphone reception. I mean, it is horrible if you have Sprint PCS. You will have to remember the address where to pick up the rider. You will not be able to start the trip until your cellphone gains the reception back halfway down the hill. These types of trips could cause you a big waste of time. But these are trips you will get if you are in Hollywood. Especially during any awards weekends such as the Oscars, Grammys, BET, or if its All-Star Weekend in LA.

It's now the end of June and its time for the BET Awards. One of the biggest events is the BET Experience Downtown Los Angeles at LA Live. So you could start there if you want to. They have a surplus of parties in the nightclubs all over the city. They also will be having an equal amount of parties and after-parties in the Hollywood Hills area. I use to think those were cool at first but not anymore. The Hills suck, but other drivers may like it. It sucks going up there most of the time due to the traffic and the wear and tear it puts on your car. You have every Uber and any other rideshare company all cramming up the same small streets. The streets are very small, and there are cars from the party and residences on the side of the road. This with all the black SUVs makes it difficult to drive through the Hills late at night. The line for picking up passengers is long, and you more than likely must make a U-turn to get back down. While waiting in the long line of vehicles to pick up a passenger, many of the passengers cancel. But don't worry and stay in line. The odds are you have to go all the way up to turn around anyway. By the time you make it to the party, you will have another rider. One dirty little tactic that many drivers may do is once they get to the party, they cancel on their rider. They then accept the next trip when they are closer to the party. This makes no sense to some, but I can understand why. After fighting up through the Hills to pick up a passenger, if they cancel when you make it up there, you are stuck having to go all the way down to the end of the line. Then you have to get back in the line, and try it all over again. So, to avoid it, some drivers cancel if they can't get the passenger on the phone. After they have cancelled and are now closer to the pickup area, they then accept the next rider. So if you are a rider and there is a long line, your Uber has a tactic. Especially if everyone that was waiting before you is still waiting.

I have tried this a couple of times but learned a lesson. I was going up to an after-party in the Hills. It was a DJ named Diplo. I get up to the Hills, and I have Joana waiting for me. After arriving halfway up and being stuck in the line of rideshare vehicles, she calls. She sounds annoyed and is impatient. She keeps asking where I am. I let her know I'm in the line of cars. She hangs up and cancels the Uber. Cool no problem with me I will pick up the next rider. I get another hit and it's Joana again. I cancel that shit and turn my app off. I then turn it back on and immediately take the next rider because I'm almost at the pickup area.

I get a call and it's the rider asking how far I am. I let her know I'm almost there and that I'm in a black Cadillac.

She says, "Ok, we see you, and we are walking to you."

I'm almost at the pickup area where they are. Four girls hop into the Cadillac. A couple of them had on some see-through lace skirts with big fake asses. I'm listening to them talk about the party and hear a familiar voice, but I can't figure out where it's from. Then all sudden out of nowhere I hear, "Are you Tyrone?"

I say yes and then she continues and says, "You canceled on me. I'm Joana."

Oh shit. "Yeah you. I remember. I thought once you canceled the first time, you didn't want to get the same Uber again."

They all are all hype now and saying yeah right, I can't believe you canceled on my girl! We are going to give you a bad rating. They gave me hell on the way back down the hill. But at the same time, they were cool about it.

The second time I did this tactic and it went bad. It was one night I dropped someone off at Chris Brown's after-party. This was at his mansion in the Hills off Mulholland. I dropped my riders off and got another rider added. Since I was already there, the new riders weren't there because they didn't expect me to arrive so fast. The LAPD asks me to move and tells me that there was no waiting.

I drive back down the hill, get in line to come back, and the rider cancels on me. I remain in line and accept the next rider when I got close to the rider pick up area. After accepting the next rider, the closer I'm getting the more nervous I'm getting because I got up here so fast. I finally get to the pickup area, and the LAPD recognizes me and asks if my riders are here this time. I say no and they say well turn your ass around again. Fucking assholes and such a waste of time. I got up to the mansion pickup area and didn't have a rider. They figured it would be a while since everyone else was outside waiting. I couldn't call with no cell reception to let them know I was already there. I haven't used that tactic sense and fuck the Hills.

You waste more than time going all the way up those hills. You waste a lot more gas because it takes a lot more power to make it up there. This why many of the residences own Range Rovers. I can smell my Cadillacs engine after I drive up there. That's how much strain on the engine it takes. Fuck that, it's not worth my engine. So after that, I made sure not to take too many trips up that way again. Although it may be a long way up, it's only a mile or couple of miles that don't add up for hell you went through. It puts you in the *Evening Crew* with all the wear and tear on your vehicle. So unless you're a groupie, avoid the Hills if you don't have a great engine.

I pick up my next rider from Play House nightclub on Hollywood Blvd. This sexy ass mixed chick with her hair out in an afro and two other nice looking chicks hop in. They and say they're going to an afterparty at Sway Lee's house, as if I know exactly where the fuck he stays. They finally put in the address, and I'm happy that I'm going to Woodland Hills. This trip is going to be over $20 bucks guaranteed! I bust a U-turn in the middle of Hollywood Blvd, turn right onto Highland, and hit the 101. On the way there, the mixed chic asks me where I'm from. I told her Texas.

She said "Me too, we are from Austin." I said cool, and then they asked if I had any coke. Right now, I'm thinking of all the times I had people offer blow and said no. Should I get involved with that shit? I should keep some in the car to supplement my income and fuck around with? Naw, kill that thought. The devil is a lie. I exit off the 101 freeway and drop them off at Sway Lee's off Ventura Blvd and I head home for that the night.

Riders have many reasons to cancel as well. They could have requested an Uber and changed their mind. Many riders cancel from not liking the person's profile pic. This could include the driver's race, gender, sexual orientation, and other reasons. This would seem as if it doesn't exist in Hollywood. But I have had many riders call after they requested an Uber and ask if I was Gay friendly.

CHAPTER VII

GAY PRIDE

Gay Pride is the busiest day period for Uber drivers besides Halloween. My experience of driving during pride is a wild one! I began early that day because the more you drive, the more money you make. Stop, rest, and grab a red bull or coffee if you must (but…it's on).

I start early before noon and begin on the Westside at the Santa Monica Pier. I pick up a group of ladies; one gets in the front, and two get in the back. I get another rider for the pool, and they all are going to Weho. Here we go, let the hustle begin. I pull up to the corner of Robertson and Santa Monica, and I let them out at the Hamburger stand across from the Abby. After they got out, I realize that the two who are in the back are men dressed in women's clothing. The whole fucking time I never looked back LMFAO! Oh well, I also didn't notice until they got out of the car what they had on. They only had on some type of see-through pantyhose and nothing underneath. I guess that's what the whispers were for during the entire commute from the pier to Santa Monica Blvd. Hey, do your thang. I don't hate. I drop the other lady in the pool off at a bar. Yes, a fucking bar that's already open, and she states that the people she is meeting have already been out partying. They were all partying since last night nonstop, and she only went home to change and get ready for pride.

On to the next trip. This time, I pick up a young Black lady who was participating in the Bisexual Float for the parade. She was cool; we had a great conversation about life and school. We both went to Cal State Dominguez Hills in Carson. After dropping her off, there is a long stare. I didn't react to it; I was too thrown off by the costume and her being in the Bisexual parade. Little did I know, she might have been for me.

Next passenger I pick up has on a costume that looks like a full-body condom. I didn't want to look too hard because I didn't know what the hell was showing and what wasn't. Fuck that. I continue to take him as close as I can to Santa Monica Blvd because by now, they are starting to block off the streets. After dropping off condom guy, I pick up my next passenger who is wearing a fucking cloth diaper! He and his boyfriend slash buddy, I guess. They were cool though, and you could tell they were on steroids. They kept asking what gym I worked out at and how much I put up on different lifts. I let them know I worked out at 24 Hr. Fitness. They mentioned they owned a gym in Silverlake. They stated that if I wanted a job and needed some extra money that I was welcome to stop by. I will pass on that for now, but I guess you can't judge a book by its cover, and you should take the time to get to know someone before judging. I drop them off and go to pick up my next rider.

I head down San Vicente to get to Melrose, and there are police, ambulances, and fire trucks everywhere. Traffic is at a standstill. I'm sitting in this car waiting and listening to music. I have no idea when they are going to let traffic move past whatever is going on. I can't see anything and be nosey, but I also can't turn and get out of here. My anxiety is kicking in. Things are starting to spin and become a blur. My heartbeat is getting faster, and I'm starting to perspire. I don't have my meds with me, which makes no sense at all. Out of the days, today is the day to have my fucking meds! I roll the windows down to get some more air and finally the cars in front of me start to move forward. I'm feeling very relieved now.

The firemen are waving us to continue and avoid the parked emergency vehicles. I finally get to where I can be nosey and see what's going on after I get past Rosewood, and I look to my left. My God, there's a dead body in the alley by the trash can and they are now covering him up. I never saw a dead body before besides at a funeral. It didn't seem to affect me that much, or so I thought.

I pull into Norms and get me some food to rest up and get energized for the rest of the day ahead of me. While I'm eating, I start to get nauseated and feel as if I'm about to throw up. I walk to the bathroom and go to the toilet and it starts coming up out of me. I start to get nervous and scared, but I'm confused because I don't know what the fuck is going on. Is this from the food? Is this from my anxiety earlier, or is this from seeing the dead body? It's all scary, but not knowing is making the shit even scarier. I look at myself in the mirror and rinse my mouth and wash my hands and face in the sink. I tell myself, *get it together, Tyrone*. After patting my face dry with the paper towels, I go straight to the register. I ask them to pull my receipt since they haven't brought it to my table yet. I pay and get the fuck out of there. I go to my car, rinse my mouth out with mouthwash, use hand sanitizer for my hand, and grab a stick of gum. I'm ready now, so let's get to it.

I turn my app on and get ready to accept a new rider, but for some reason I turn it back off. The next thing I know, I'm at home sleep. I don't know how I got there and don't remember driving. I get up and check for the time on my phone and it's dead. I walk in the kitchen and look at the microwave it's almost 10 pm. Its as if I got drunk partying and had a blackout. But I haven't been partying nor have I been drinking. I plug my phone up to charge it and get into the shower and get ready for the second round.

CHAPTER VIII

HEAD GAMES & NOT QUITE VOMIT

I finally get ready to drive later than I expected at a little before midnight. Upon starting to drive, I start to get a nervous feeling in my stomach again. I decide to take it easy tonight, so I started around Studio City and NoHo. I had the understanding that I would end up in Hollywood/WeHo later but wasn't up to driving straight into the shit.

I get my first hit at a bar called Games and Dames in North Hollywood. Upon arriving, I see my rider flagging me down. He was a short Mexican male with glasses. He asks if it's ok to sit in the front. I said cool, I don't mind. Upon sitting in the front, he immediately asks how my night has been going. I mentioned that I started and that it was my first trip. He then continues to ask me if I'm hungry and if I would like some tacos. I said no thank you. I just got out of the shower and brushed my teeth. There was no way that I was going to eat some tacos and continue driving after that.

The dude keeps asking and says that he is buying as if I gave a fuck. I had to tell him again no thank you, I'm good. "Well why not?" He says again, "I'm buying."

Bruh I don't need you to buy me anything I'm good. This dude is about to get on my fucking nerves, and he picked the wrong night to fuck around. He continues about how he is paying for it, and that I should at least get the tacos and take them with me. By now, I'm realizing what this is about and that this dude likes me. It didn't dawn on me before, but I get why he asked to sit in the front. I was thinking it's more comfortable to sit in the front as many other riders do. Some riders aren't comfortable riding in the back as if they are in a limo. Some think it's safer in the front seat for some reason. I get a little more assertive and let the dude know what time it was with me and that I was good. He discontinued asking, and I dropped his ass off. Damn, now I get what women may go through. Poor ladies.

My next pick up is in NoHo where I pick up a guy and his girlfriend. Luckily for me they are going to Astro Burger in WeHo on Santa Monica Blvd. I ask them if they think it's open and that I may or may not be able to drop them off there due to everything being blocked off.

"Don't worry. Anywhere around there is ok, and we will walk the rest."

As I'm driving down the 101-freeway getting ready to exit Highland, I hear some moaning as if someone is getting some pleasure. I'm a bit confused because I know they aren't fucking, at least not that fast. I look at my review and I see the dude head bobbing up and down and the chick is moaning. I'm still confused. How is the dude looking like he is sucking dick, but the chick is moaning? Isn't this supposed to be the other way around? This shit is throwing me off. The chick looks a little butch, maybe a dyke, but I don't understand what the fuck is going on back there. After looking a little closer, this dyke chick got this dude sucking her strap- on. She grabbing the dude by the back of the head as if he is the bitch. I kept driving. Shit, what could I say? I drop them off behind the Astro Burger, she says thanks for the ride, and I kept it moving.

The app goes off again, and I turn right back around across the street from Astro Burger. I pull over to Fat Burger and pick up a brother from New York. He was cool and dressed in some jean shorts, a collared shirt, and some Timberland boots. He is going to Rage, and I tell him I will get him as close as I can through the alleys.

I let him out, and when he exits he smiles and says, "Well, wish me luck!"

I said, "Good luck, man. You got this."

I feel as if I'm the father that dropped his son off at prom. It is a good feeling, but short-lived because the app is on fire.

My next trip is going to be a difficult one. The Abby is a bitch to get to, but it's a surge, and it may be worth it. I make it to Melrose and drive up Robertson. I find a way to park on the side the road across for Boss nova. The riders call me and ask me where I'm at, and I tell them. They find me, and as I had already planned for, they are carrying someone. I don't mind driving drunk people, especially if they pass out. It's the rude and disrespectful drunks or the ones that vomit that I have a problem with. They drop their buddy off in the back seat and take off back towards the Abby. They aren't done for the night, so they got an Uber for their friend to send his ass off so they could continue partying.

I take off and fight to get out of traffic. I double back around to Santa Monica Blvd. and finally to the 405 freeway. I exit and get to Playa Del Rey where the rider's destination is. Once I get onto Culver Blvd from Lincoln, I'm driving through the swamps. This dude gets up and starts to open the door while the car is moving.

He starts to get out of the car, and I yell, "Stop man! Get the fuck back in the car!"

I reach back, grab him by the back of his shirt collar, and snatch him back in the car. I do all this while slowing the car down and pulling over to the side of the road. After I pull over, I go around to the back seat and he passes back out. I push him up, put his seat belt back on, and shut the door. I get back in the car and I lock the door. Finally, I start back driving again for the second time to this guy's destination. He gets up again and starts fighting to get out of his seat belt. Dude is trying to vomit from the bottom of his core to the top of his lungs. He is making this squealing noise that reminds me of a fucking pig or wild hogs back in Texas. This shit is funny as fuck to me. This guy is struggling to get something up out of him but it's not working. The more he wants the shit to come up, the louder he starts squealing. Poor fellow. I can't help but think how much of what he had to drink and what drug he was on.

He reminded me of a passenger that I had picked up one night in Hollywood. This was the first time a rider scared me. He sat in the front seat, and his tongue kept moving around in his mouth. His jaws and mouth were making chewing-like sucking movements. Dude kept chewing as if he ate grass like a cow with a dry mouth. It was weird at first, but after I figured he was on something, it put me a little more at ease.

The person I have in the back now reminds me of him, only a drunken version. Part of me was very concerned for him and thought that I should take the guy to a hospital or call 911. The squealing is getting more intense, this guy is dry heaving his ass off. I can't help but be a little happy at the fact that nothing coming up. For me, that means at least my car will stay clean.

I make it to the rider's destination, and by now, he has passed back out. I park at the building that's on the app as his destination and go around to the back seat to get him up. The rider won't wake up, and he has a little spit from all the dry heaving on his shirt, pants, and seat. I take a picture of him sitting in my backseat passed out in the seat belt with the spit upon his clothes and my backseat. I send the report along with the photos to Uber, then I continue to try and get the guy awake and out of my car. This is wasting my time; there is plenty of money out there tonight.

I conclude that I am going to have to call an ambulance for the poor guy. I go to the front seat to grab my phone. While doing so, he wakes up and rushes to the gate of his building as if he was a hostage or something. I tried to calm him down and let him know his friends got an Uber for him, but he was too frightened to hear anything I had to say. Why am I here? Didn't I want this dude out of my car? I see him struggling at the gate with putting in the key code. Not my problem. My job complete, I'm out.

I pull out from his building parking lot, park, and begin wiping down my seats and spraying the new car air freshener. I keep the windows down and drive off toward Lincoln, and then I get a hit form LMU. I like driving up to LMU. It's beautiful, plus I know the gate guard Reggie. Reggie works the gate late night and early morning, and he owns the barbershop I get my haircut at. I get up to the gate and Reggie is there. We say what's up and rap a little bit, then I head up the hill to pick up my passenger. They are going to the airport, so here I am about to run the track again.

It's almost four in the morning. That hog squealing, dry heaving guy from Pride cost me a lot of money. I still haven't heard from Uber yet about the cleaning fee. I make it to the airport and drop of the riders from LMU, and by the time I do, the cleaning fee adds to my fare. $140 for the trip plus cleaning fee. A nice night I'd say.

I decide not to run the track due to becoming a little tired. I kept my app on and figured I would take the next run from either Culver City or Inglewood.

My app goes off, and Culver City it is. I ended up getting off the freeway going through some alley to arrive at a warehouse. Someone must be getting home from work, so this should be a short trip. Then I could go in for the day. As I pull up closer to the warehouse, I see a bunch of people in costume. It looks as if they have been filming a scene from some post-apocalyptic film. I could have sworn that I have been on the scene as a background extra all over again. A group of people come up to me in what I thought was their wardrobes for the post-apocalyptic film. They ask me if I was Uber. I stated yes get on in. They begin piling in one at a time. It was at least 4 of them. One White guy in the front, and two guys, one White and one Black guy with a British accent, in the back. There is also one White girl in the back with them.

I begin to ask if they were filming and they say "Huh? No."

Then out of nowhere, the White guy in the backseat says, "Whoa man, cool shirt!"

I was like, "Ok, thank you."

The White girl and the Black guy in the back both began to comment on how cool and nice my shirt was. Now, mind you I only had on a burgundy collared shirt that had a nice shine to it. They all kept complimenting my shirt on how beautiful the color was.

The White guy in the front proceeds to ask me how long I have been driving and asks if I needed a bump.

I say, "No, I don't do coke."

He then proceeds to ask if I did mushrooms and pulls out about a half-pound or more of mushrooms from his backpack. By now I'm starting to understand why they were complimenting on the color of my shirt. These guys are tripping on mushrooms or some type of psychedelic. They're not even actors; this is the shit they are wearing to party in. This is their regular clothes, what the fuck! So, I decline on the mushrooms and continue driving. I end up dropping them off at the Santa Monica Hotel.

I take my next trip, which is another airport run. Ok, this is my last trip. It's already after 5 am, and I have been up driving since before midnight. But I got another run in me. I take my next rider to the airport, and I am about to drop them off when they say that there is a new iPhone in the back seat.

"Thanks for letting me know. I will contact the last riders and see if it's theirs."

I remember dropping the last riders at the Santa Monica hotel and go back there since it's on the way back to the Valley. I grab the phone and take it with me. I know which room they're in because I can hear the Black guy's British accent. I knock on the door with my left hand and the phone in my right hand. They open the door, and I begin to ask if someone lost a phone. Before I could say anything they immediately zoomed in on the phone in my right hand. They all start rushing towards me giving me hugs and high fives. I hand them the phone and they continue trying to give me cocaine and mushrooms that continue to decline.

But now, I'm starting to think of those fine ass chicks from Texas. How this may be a connection and somewhat of a blessing. They continued to insist, but I continued to decline. Finally after them continuing to offer me things, we all settled on me going to a bonfire with them the next day. We exchanged numbers, and I continued home to the Valley. But for some reason, I couldn't stop thinking of the cocaine and the bitches.

CHAPTER VIIII

THE GENESIS OF A HUSTLER

I said I didn't want to sell dope. I better stay away. Here I go facing my past all over again. I joined the military to stay away from the shit. But the dope game is calling me. The opportunity for more income accelerated with bad bitches is an offer I can't refuse.

I tried doing things the right way, but I can't shake the young hustler in me.

I fought against myself at the beginning of driving. The app went off at the spot I was inputting my information, had it not I may not have been driving all this time. Driving has its positives and negatives and will bring a lot out of you. You will learn to deal with people all over again. From badass kids, traffic, asked out for tacos by a guy, and seeing your first dead body.

My anxiety let me know it was with me many times in traffic with people. I learned how to manage it along with taking my medication before driving. I also learned a lot about people in general. Uber provided an opportunity for me to discover different parts of myself. The part that was anxious in traffic around people. The part that was a procrastinator and didn't complete the tasks that I started. The part of me that still had childhood fantasies that wanted to be played out.

My therapist once told me that sometimes during stress and anxiety the brain goes back to a time it was secure. That time for me was when I sold drugs as a hustler before the military. It only makes sense now why I'm so attracted to it. If I could have a little coke in the car with me while I was driving after the clubs it could be beneficial. The cops aren't tripping, they know that if the car is an Uber it at least has a license, registration, and insurance. It would be a waste to pull the car over, besides they got fights and shootings they're occupied with. This way I would be secure and still be able to pursue my dream of acting in the process. All the time I spent up in those Hills at the mansion parties all provided income opportunities for me. This all at the expense of my engine of course. After weighing the pros and cons of driving and considering the wear and tear it isn't worth it. The amount of driving that you have to do at the expense of the engine combined with some of the shit you have to deal with. This doesn't weigh out. But it is if you are not only driving and have another agenda. I guess I will think about it?

I got the stoner's that invited me to the bonfire. Maybe that's the play? I guess I could at least go, and if they don't have it I know someone at the bonfire will. This is all a risk, but so was moving to Hollywood in the first place. Fuck It.

To be continued...

P.M. PUBLISHING

At P.M. Publishing we focus on new authors that have emphasis in urban and creative non-fiction. We hope you found this E-Book interesting an worth your time. If there was new thoughts or ideas about humanity please feel free to leave an honest review.

Stay connected as we will ne publishing new content including the sequel and final of Anxious Uber Driver.

You can get latest news from our email list.

https://mailchi.mp/e2b628dea061/pmpublishing

Connect on Instagram @ pm_publishing

www.ingramcontent.com/pod-product-compliance
Lightning Source LLC
Chambersburg PA
CBHW051417250726
48655CB00003B/1097